# practical
# centering

## Books by Larkin Barnett

*Practical Pilates Using Imagery*
a book for adults featuring dancers
from the Miami City Ballet

*Pilates and Calisthenics for Children*

*Creative Yoga for Children*

*On a Lark: Creative Movement for Children*

*All available from:*
Lorenz Educational Press,
c/o the Lorenz Corporation
501 East Third Street, Box 802
Dayton, OH 45401-0802
www.LorenzEducationalPress.com
1-800-444-1144

# practical
# centering

*exercises to **energize your chakras***
*for relaxation, vitality, and health*

## LARKIN BARNETT

Foreword by Dr. Gregory Loewen, Pulmonary Oncology
and Dr. Madeline Singer, PhD, Clinical Hypnotherapy

THEOSOPHICAL PUBLISHING HOUSE
WHEATON, ILLINOIS • CHENNAI, INDIA

Quest Books
Theosophical Publishing House
P. O. Box 270
Wheaton, IL 60187-0270

www.questbooks.net

Book design and typesetting by Drew Stevens

Library of Congress Cataloging-in-Publication Data

Barnett, Larkin.
    Practical centering: exercises to energize your chakras for relaxation, vitality, and health / Larkin Barnett; foreword by Gregory Loewen and Madeline Singer.—1st. Quest ed.
    p.    cm.
ISBN 978-0-8356-0903-6
1. Chakras.  2. Vitality.  3. Health.  I. Title.
RZ999.B265 2012
615.8'52—dc23                              2011041802

Printed in the United States of America
5   4   3   2      *   12   13   14   15   16

*For my parents,*
*Dr. Robert Peter Barnett and*
*Suzanne Patricia Barnett*

*For my grandparents,*
*Dr. William Kress McIntyre and*
*Mary Rose McIntyre*
*and*
*Dr. Edwin Judge Barnett and*
*Agnes Virginia Barnett*

# Table of Contents

# Foreword: Blending Western and Eastern Traditions

**Dr. Gregory Loewen, Pulmonary Oncology Specialist, and Dr. Madeline Singer, PhD, Clinical Hypnotherapy**

## *View from the West*

**Dr. Gregory Loewen, Pulmonary Oncology Specialist**

Two patients visit the lung doctor. Both take a pulmonary function test to measure the strength of their breathing. Both tests are abnormal and show the same lung condition. The patients have virtually identical test results. The columns of numbers suggest the degree of disability should be identical. Here is the surprise: One patient is profoundly short of breath, is unable to work, and is barely able to function. The other patient has breathing symptoms but continues to function and works full time. What causes such a difference in breathing?

For these two patients, the difference could be in how each *thinks* about his or her breathing. How we think about our breathing really matters and directly affects our exercise capacity, stamina, and fitness.

In *Practical Centering*, Larkin correctly implies that there are many variables, including lung disease that profoundly affect our breathing. They include shallow-breathing habits, traumatic events, memories, and even the messages that we send to ourselves about these events. The very messages that we tell ourselves matter, too.

In Larkin's Foundation Formula, she describes the science of breathing with words and anatomy-based images of muscle groups. This provides the reader renewed core vitality and peaceful mental interludes. Her Foundation Formula contains pursed-lip breathing, which is an essential technique used by doctors who treat patients with shortness of breath, particularly from chronic obstructive pulmonary disease (COPD). The pursed-lip technique is widely used by respiratory therapists. It opens airways for the more efficient release of carbon dioxide and improves oxygenation. If you are under a doctor's care for COPD, asthma, or any other lung condition, it is a good idea to make sure your doctor has determined you are stable enough to do yogic breath work. If your breathing seems to be worsening with any exercise, contact your doctor.

Larkin's Three-Dimensional Balloon Breathing, gentle stretching, and yogic techniques are helpful for most lung conditions and can significantly improve pulmonary symptoms. There is growing evidence that these kinds of techniques improve the quality of life and lung function in patients with COPD.

Chakras are ancient, non-Western concepts demonstrating the physical and spiritual contact points in the human body. The chakra model does not contradict modern science but complements Western understanding of how our bodies function.

Using innovative physical exercises, colorful words, and visual imagery, Larkin makes complex breathing concepts simple to change your life one conscious breath at a time. In her Chakra Rocking Massage, she draws the participant through powerful spiritual exercises that transcend breathing. The net effect of Larkin's work is a new, integrative adaptation of breathing strategies, from both an Eastern and a Western perspective. With inspiration, humor, and artistry, her exercises guide you towards centeredness and healing.

## View from the East
### Dr. Madeline Singer, PhD, Clinical Hypnotherapy

**A**chieving balance in today's hectic world is challenging. When mind, body, and spirit are in harmony, you create true peace.

Time is precious. Each week has 168 hours, 10,080 minutes, or 604,800 seconds. As we age, time flies, and the older we get, the faster it flies away. *Practical Centering* is a system that elevates our energy to accomplish our goals.

We focus on our health when it is not optimal. The pressure of a fast-paced lifestyle takes its toll. Thoughts directed by the unconscious mind are often rigid old patterns of thinking. A pattern of tightness in the muscles can begin in the mind. The root cause may be illness, surgery, accidents, abuse, emotional trauma, daily stress, poor movement habits, or even one's choice of sport or fitness. The expression "When you have your health, you are truly rich" is paramount today. *Practical Centering* teaches you how to turn inward to build body and mind awareness through innovative, efficient breathing techniques and empowering exercises.

It only requires a few minutes to achieve efficient breathing through imagery, massage, chakra color, affirmations, progressive relaxation, meditation, and true core strength. Larkin's Chakra Rocking Massage contains rhythmic movement of the body working as a unit. These repetitive, gentle motions are reminiscent of being rocked in a cradle—they are calming, soothing, and tension releasing.

*Practical Centering* enhances physical, mental, and emotional balance. The Chakra Rocking Massage dissipates muscular tension. Muscles have less congestion and toxicity, allowing energy to move more freely throughout the body. Focusing upon breathing, imagery, color, and affirmations reduces the debilitating effects of daily stress.

Larkin's exercises create a vacation experience. You cultivate the mind/body connection to discover efficient ways to handle life's tasks with ease. Since we draw to us what we think, the power of our mind/body connection can be a defense against illness or a "steering wheel" for the ultimate immune booster. The self-massage and breathing improve blood and lymphatic circulation, which heightens tissue nutrition and metabolism. The body acts like a natural pharmacy as it flushes away waste products more thoroughly. The exercises train your nervous system to sustain longer interludes of peace.

# Acknowledgments

When I was a child, my loving father and mother died separately, both at the age of forty, due to stress-related circumstances. Their passing knocked the wind out of me. As with so many others faced with a life-altering event, I unconsciously developed the habit of shallow chest breathing. When I attended modern dance classes in college, my poor respiratory habits put me at a distinct disadvantage, as compared with other students. My complexion was red, my stamina insufficient, and my movements were restricted as I endeavored to excel in my chosen field. I experienced a breakthrough from my dance professor, Eija Celli, who introduced me to the work of the renowned architect and movement theorist Rudolf von Laban. His spatial concepts led to the development of my Three-Dimensional Breathing. One day while choreographing, I made an important discovery: It is possible to direct one's intake of air into the vertical, horizontal, sagittal, or three-dimensional spatial regions located within the body.

I'd also like to thank my graduate-level dance kinesiology professor, Patrice Griffen. Patrice was responsible for challenging me to analyze the visual imagery teaching cues used in technique class. Visual imagery helps dancers execute movements with more efficiency, safety, and artistic expression. You are holding a book that uses my anatomy-based visual imagery mind/body exercises because of this inspiration.

I also created my Chakra Rocking Massage Exercises thanks, in part, to the inspiration of a client who'd spent years studying yoga. She challenged me by saying, "I bet the seven Rocking Massage Exercises each relate to a specific chakra." At that period in my modern dance career, all I knew was that the Rocking Massage movements had kept me injury-free.

I'm grateful to my students at Fitness First in Arlington, Massachusetts. While doing high-impact aerobics in the early eighties, and in order to protect their bodies, I created my core abdominal Foundation Formula. Since then, hundreds of people have made it a part of their daily lives, exercise programs, sports, dance, martial arts, or physical therapy. By focusing on making it a daily habit, they build core potential while improving their functional movement patterns.

I'd also like to thank my motivational students over the past decades for advocating the value of the Foundation Formula and sharing how they gained mastery rather than depletion during illness, injury, and severe stress. This book adds *color* to the Foundation Formula for more safety and success.

I was fortunate to work at Canyon Ranch Spa with actors, opera singers, and Olympic athletes who all rely, professionally, on the power of consciously controlled, deep diaphragmatic breathing. They encouraged me to document my techniques. I'd like to give special thanks to my copy editor, Linda Tangredi, and to my graphic arts designer, Kristen Morales, for her exercise illustrations. Thank you also to my editors Joanne Asala and Sharron Dorr. Thanks to physical therapist David Owan for his safety guidelines.

Finally, I'd like to thank you, the reader, for your interest in this book. Enjoy strengthening your core, relaxing your body, and quieting your mind as you savor inner awareness. I hope the ingredients contained in this book help you to feel centered while becoming the best part of your day!

# Introduction

In many ways, *Practical Centering* needs no introduction. These practical exercises are convenient enough to fit into your lifestyle, instead of forcing you to fit the exercises into a routine.

Don't feel obligated to read or use the exercises in this book from start to finish. The chapters do build on one another, but feel free to skip around.

The beginning pages of the book will take you through a basic understanding of visualization, your chakra energetic system, and the self-massage motion. The chakra recipe cards in chapter two provide a solid foundation for awareness of your chakras. You're encouraged to practice the massage motion before you implement it in the actual exercises.

Train your breathing mechanism every day. Perform both the deep relaxation diaphragmatic breathing and the dynamic core control breathing anytime, anywhere, throughout your daily routine—and practice often.

Practice the other exercises based on your schedule, as well as how your body feels. Your own stress and energy levels will let you know when to treat yourself to a self-massage. At least once a week, enjoy a massage. You can stretch and meditate for a bit every day. You may find that progressive relaxation helps you to meditate or fall asleep at night.

The exercises take only minutes. It is enjoyable to practice the relaxation breathing with your massage. You will be so relaxed that you naturally go right into meditation. After meditation, you may want to stretch and do progressive relaxation before getting up from a lying down position.

The possibilities are endless because the exercises are versatile and practical. Enjoy mixing them up. They will make you feel so good that exercising will be the best part of your day.

# 1

# Visual Imagery, Consciously-controlled Breathing, and the Mind/Body Connection

The use of visual imagery and consciously-controlled breathing is the most direct pathway to your mind/body connection. When we use visual imagery, we construct a mental picture to accomplish a physical task. Visualize what you see in your mind's eye to create an image to send to your body. "Feel" it with one or all of your senses. Breathing is the only involuntary system of the body that we can consciously control. For most of us, this system is relatively dormant, yet learning to utilize it is the key to radiant health.

Healthy people understand that our minds play a critical role in our physical well-being. You will discover that the power of the mind is the key to your most healthy body.

Olympic athletes use visualization to imagine the "perfect execution" of their event. While visualizing, athletes simultaneously "feel" their bodies performing. If you can see it and can feel it, you can transform your body.

Use this book to become a champion in your own life. A champion's inner voice is positive, encouraging, and instructive. Visualization is a powerful way to become absorbed in the movement experience and to suppress negative emotion. When performing the exercises in this book, avoid distractions. Think about visual imagery and breathing. Paint a picture in your mind that you can see, and then feel it with your body. Don't let negative thoughts creep into your consciousness. The reward will be deep relaxation and a heightened sense of being alive.

Three-Dimensional Balloon Breathing and the core abdominal Foundation Formula, as outlined in chapters six and ten, provide completely portable and instant stress management. You learn techniques you can do anytime, anywhere—in a traffic jam, at your desk, at a doctor's office, in your hotel room, during errands and chores, or on an airplane.

Imagine the possibilities! You're three hours into a long flight from Los Angeles to New York. Your back is sore, and your legs begin to cramp. You can practice Three-Dimensional

Balloon Breathing and the Foundation Formula in combination with your chakra color imagery, and in only a few seconds, you begin to feel the tension melt away. Later, performing the Chakra Rocking Massage Exercises when you reach your destination is like taking a mini-vacation.

We seldom allow ourselves to pause our busy lives long enough to turn our attention inward. Disconnecting from our physical body allows stress to erode our health. To correct this problem, you can easily use the core abdominal Foundation Formula when you get in and out of a car, chair, or bed, while you are climbing stairs, and while you are walking. You will cause less wear and tear to your body, and in many cases, find you are moving in a more youthful manner.

You can reprogram your mind/body connection and make many positive changes. The Foundation Formula utilizes the mind/body connection to improve your body's ability to move with ease and efficiency and significantly improve your posture. You will experience fewer aches and pains and have an increased ability to cope with stress.

## The ABC—Action, Belief, Consequence Exercise

Many people believe that the mind and body are at odds. Changing the "inner messages" you give yourself by consciously choosing how you respond to stress is the first step in bringing the mind and body together as a team.

**A**ction: Begin by picturing a stressful action that happened recently. What was your emotional response to that action? Were you anxious, frustrated, or angry?

**B**elief: What were your beliefs about that event?

**C**onsequence: What were the consequences or the physiological response of your beliefs? Did you feel your heart rate elevate or your shoulders tense, or did you develop a headache?

We can't always control the stress going on around us. You can learn to modify your internal reaction to stress by interrupting your response between step one, the action, and step two, the belief. More importantly, that choice changes your habitual physiological response or consequence that breaks down your body.

You will find yourself less reactive to stressful circumstances, needing to count to ten less often. For immediate physiological and mood changes, reprogram your stress response using the affirmations, breathing, and core exercises in the book. We take our cars in for routine service. Your own "vehicle," your body, requires body maintenance, too. These body-care routines cultivate awareness by guiding you to habitually choose to focus on what's going on within you even while on the run.

Breathing and contracting your deep abdominals are your daily "road map" to feeling fit. Make moving from your core abdominals a constant priority while lifting heavy objects, climbing stairs, or anytime you move. Adding the core abdominal Foundation Formula is a lifestyle choice as important as getting plenty of water and rest. It provides stability for the spine and takes the pressure off the joints.

You learn how to implement mastery over your energy levels instead of depletion. This comes from discovering the body's breathing spaces, working your diaphragm, and contracting your abdominal muscles. These tools are for real life and change your inner stress-response messages. Consistent practice builds a "breath savings account" that accrues health dividends for all systems of the body.

Close your eyes and disentangle yourself from outside concerns—and even from the chatter of the mind—to calm down your nervous system. Turn your focus inward and recharge your batteries with a quick breathing break. You can do it behind a closed door at your office, during airplane travel, or just while walking. You will notice more energy and better concentration through conscious breathing. Anxiety and worry cause our bodies to go on alert. These breathing techniques provide relaxation for mind and body.

The Chakra Rocking Massage improves tissue health, suppleness, and posture. The gentle body maintenance massage helps to resolve muscle soreness, aches, and discomfort we think we must live with. The tools in this book reinforce a healthy relationship to your nervous system for a life with more vitality and peace.

## Anchor Your Exercises with Color Imagery

You will increase body awareness through visualizing vibrant colors in conjunction with visual images. Color imagery, with its profound impact on the nervous system, helps you to reach your goals. Color imagery allows more intake of air during Three-Dimensional Balloon Breathing, deeper abdominal contractions during the Foundation Formula, and more supple muscles in the Chakra Rocking Massage. You will also release habitually tight muscles during Progressive Relaxation.

Allow color to permeate the body maintenance exercises. The goal of the Foundation Formula is to contract the deep abdominals. Color helps identify the elusive stomach muscles and intensify your physical ability to contract them. Color helps you to let go, unwind, and enjoy the physical sensation of loose, supple, and toned muscles. Your reward is a calm mind and a joyful spirit.

# 2

# What Are Chakras?

C hakras are spinning vortices of energy located along the spine. Positioned from the tailbone to the crown of the head, they are part of your energetic anatomy. The vertical alignment of the chakras symbolizes the journey from the material world upward to the divine.

There are references to the chakras in the Vedas, ancient Hindu texts of knowledge, which date from 2,000 to 600 B.C. The chakras came to be one of the integral parts of yoga philosophy and are bridges to higher consciousness; meditation can awaken these energy centers.

Wherever dynamic energies come together in nature, they form spinning circular patterns, or vortices. On a small scale, this becomes apparent as tiny spirals on the surface of streams; on a large scale, in the cloud systems that create cyclones. The seers of ancient India perceived similar vortices within the energy of the human body. The human body has seven of these energy or power centers. Derived from the Sanskrit word for "wheel," chakras spin like wheels of colored light.

In the journey to achieve personal power, each chakra defines and adds a dimension to the purpose of life and helps achieve insight and balance. This sacred ancient imagery is accurate in its symbolic depiction of an individual's maturation.

## Chakras—Colors, Centers, and Energy

Although not visible to the naked eye, the seven chakras are associated with seven colors. They are red (survival), orange (pleasure), yellow (power), green (love), blue (self-expression), indigo (intuition), and violet (spirituality). Visualize the chakras as you would a rainbow or sunlight that streams through stained glass, bright but transparent. The human body at its most basic level is pure energy. Imagine your spectrum of chakra colors and feel what it is like to touch your energy system. Through the chakras, you can discover a part of your anatomy that you didn't know existed and use it to enhance your well-being and health.

In this book, you will learn to maximize chakras and use their associations to chart your progress. As you experience each chakra exercise, you will heighten your senses and connect to a calm state that resides within you. Life lessons, or energetic associations, have representation in the seven chakra centers. The first three chakras embody specific spiritual life lessons in the material world. The next four higher chakras suggest the spiritual ascension.

**MATERIAL WORLD**

> **First Chakra:** Material and physical world
> **Second Chakra:** Creation, work, relationships, and emotions
> **Third Chakra:** Self-empowerment, mind, and personality

**SPIRITUAL ASCENSION**

> **Fourth Chakra:** Love, compassion, and forgiveness
> **Fifth Chakra:** Will and self-expression
> **Sixth Chakra:** Intuition, insight, and wisdom
> **Seventh Chakra:** Spirituality

The chakras reside just beyond the boundary of your physical body. They link with your physical body in the following seven locations:

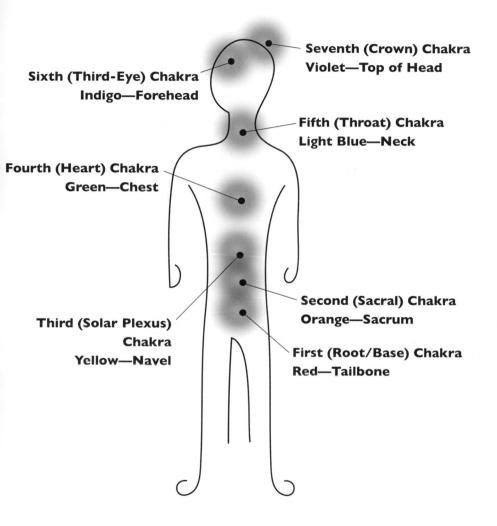

Seventh (Crown) Chakra
Violet—Top of Head

Sixth (Third-Eye) Chakra
Indigo—Forehead

Fifth (Throat) Chakra
Light Blue—Neck

Fourth (Heart) Chakra
Green—Chest

Second (Sacral) Chakra
Orange—Sacrum

Third (Solar Plexus)
Chakra
Yellow—Navel

First (Root/Base) Chakra
Red—Tailbone

## Chakra Ingredients for Your Mind/Body Experience

While you learn to enhance your mind/body experience practicing the Chakra Rocking Massage Exercises, you will focus on the unique elements of the chakras (chapter five). This is like stirring in the correct ingredients to make your favorite recipe complete. As you practice, you will remember each important ingredient and your "recipe" will become second nature. The ingredients for your experience include color, location, life lesson, keywords, elements, senses, glands, emotions, and affirmations. Glands are like chemical messengers, and each gland relates to a particular chakra.

# The Root/Base (First) Chakra

## Ingredients

**Color:** Red. *Breathe in the color and visualize it moving around your tailbone.*

**Location:** Base of your tailbone

**Life Lessons:** Survival/physical, basic body needs

**Keyword:** Acceptance

**Element:** Earth

**Sense:** Smell

**Gland:** Adrenals. *The adrenal glands secrete hormones essential for our primitive "fight or flight" response.*

**Feelings/Emotions:** Feeling safe and secure

**Affirmations:** "I am grounded and supported in all areas of my life. I feel worthy of abundance."

# The Sacral (Second) Chakra

## Ingredients

**Color:**  Orange. *Breathe in the color and visualize it moving around your hips.*

**Location:**  Pelvic area/lower abdomen

**Life Lessons:**  Emotion, pleasure, sensuality

**Keyword:**  Sweetness

**Element:**  Water

**Sense:**  Taste

**Gland:**  Ovaries/testes.

**Feelings/Emotions:**  Delight in the senses

**Affirmations:**  "I am enjoying and appreciating the goodness of life, including my relationships."

# The Solar Plexus (Third) Chakra

## Ingredients

**Color:** Yellow. *Breathe in the color and visualize it moving around your navel.*

**Location:** Solar plexus, between navel and base of sternum

**Life Lesson:** Mental/true inner personal power

**Keywords:** Self-respect, confidence, discipline

**Element:** Fire

**Sense:** Sight

**Glands:** Pancreas, adrenals. *Listen to your inner guidance and honor your "gut feelings."*

**Feeling/Emotion:** Courage

**Affirmations:** "I am powerful and I am cultivating more courage. I enlist cooperation and support when needed."

## RECIPE CARD 4

# The Heart (Fourth) Chakra

## Ingredients

**Color:** Green. *Breathe in the color and visualize it moving around the heart.*

**Location:** Heart, center of chest

**Life Lesson:** Growth through love

**Keywords:** Body, spirit, harmony, trust

**Element:** Air

**Sense:** Touch

**Gland:** Thymus

**Feelings/Emotions:** Forgiveness, compassion, nurturing

**Affirmations:** "I am unconditional love. Love is the strongest force in the universe."

## RECIPE CARD 5

# The Throat (Fifth) Chakra

## Ingredients

**Color:** Blue. *Breathe in the color and visualize it moving around your throat.*

**Location:** Throat, neck

**Life Lessons:** Communication, self-expression, listening to the wisdom from within, the stillness that lies between your thoughts

**Keywords:** Listening, speaking

**Element:** Ether

**Sense:** Hearing

**Glands:** Thyroid, parathyroid

**Feelings/Emotions:** Kindness, thoughtfulness

**Affirmations** "I am the inspired wisdom within you. I have the gift of a childlike curiosity for life."

## RECIPE CARD 6

# The Third-Eye (Sixth) Chakra

## Ingredients

**Color:** Indigo. *Breathe in the color and visualize it moving around your forehead.*

**Location:** Forehead, above and between the eyebrows

**Life Lesson:** Blossoming of intuition

**Keywords:** Inner vision

**Element:** Light

**Senses:** Sixth sense, intuition

**Glands:** Pituitary, hypothalamus

**Feelings/Emotions:** Tranquility, generosity

**Affirmations:** "I use my imagery and visualization. I renew my energy in nature. I am grateful for easy and effortless action. I am observing the magic of life."

## RECIPE CARD 7

# The Crown (Seventh) Chakra

## Ingredients

**Color:** Violet. *Breathe in the color violet and visualize it moving around the crown of your head.*

**Location:** Crown/top of head

**Life Lessons:** Acceptance of a higher guidance, spirituality

**Keywords:** Co-creation, transcendence, infinite possibilities, gratitude

**Element:** Cosmic energy

**Sense:** Faith beyond the senses

**Gland:** Pineal

**Feelings/Emotions:** Selflessness, joy, happiness

**Affirmations:** "I am at peace. I am compassionate and enjoy helping others."

# 3

# Introduction to the Chakra Rocking Massage—The Body/Chakra Connection

The Chakra Rocking Massage Exercises are helpful re-alignment/release techniques that offer a practical, user-friendly way to physically relax and soothe you mentally and emotionally. Adding breath and chakra color imagery deepens muscle relaxation while calming the mind. When the seven chakras are in balance, particular parts of the body achieve perfect functioning. Meditation awakens the chakra energy centers. The Chakra Rocking Massage is a movement meditation that shifts your focus from outside concerns while improving your body awareness.

The Chakra Rocking Massage keeps energy flowing freely throughout the body and provides an improved state of health. Energy blockages within the body lead to *dis*-ease that is reflected in the chakra energetic system. The self-massage helps avoid manifesting physical ailments that begin at an energetic level. Self-massage improves blood and lymphatic circulation and flushes waste products. The Chakra Rocking

Massage realigns your body so you experience fewer aches and less discomfort. The gentle rocking sensation coordinates the mind/body to cultivate a sense of peace.

Supporting the belief that the chakras spin at seven distinct locations along the spine, the massage-like motion rocks the body as a unit from the tailbone to the crown of the head. The exercises provide a physical outlet to reflect upon each chakra. Refer to the chakra recipe cards in chapter two to enrich your experience.

The mind, rather than the sense organs, was the traditional tool for accessing, exploring, and balancing the energy of each chakra. The Chakra Rocking Massage movement patterns allow you to use the mind and body connection. The seven distinct body positions require different muscle memory and coordination patterns. Your goal is to visualize your interconnecting chakra wheels spinning in harmony while rocking. Focus also on the colors, affirmations, and life lessons.

## Benefits of the Chakra Rocking Massage

The massage provides deeply relaxing realignment movements that improve your posture. They decompress the spine by elongating the trunk muscles. The subtle movements activate the synovial fluid that lubricates the joints. They relax the neck, the shoulders, and the back muscles, which helps to minimize headaches and back discomfort. They alleviate digestive and sleep problems.

- Consistent practice helps significantly reduce muscular tension that builds up due to poor posture, repetitive movements, and stress. Layer after layer of muscular tightness dissipates, from the tips of your toes to the top of your head. This realigns your entire body as a unit.

- Self-massage improves the circulation of oxygen, and the energy flows freely throughout the body, preventing physical problems or emotional stress. The Chakra Rocking

Massage is synonymous with the chakra energy system in the sense that it assists uninhibited flow of energy throughout the body. This establishes a vital link to our physical well-being.

- The Chakra Rocking Massage manages stress through self-massage, efficient breathing, better alignment, and visual imagery. Due to the mind/body connection, negative emotions and thought patterns contribute to tight muscles. It is typical for intense feelings to surface as you shed layers of muscular tension. Consistent practice will reward you with a relaxed body, calm mind, and renewed spirit.

- The Chakra Rocking Massage promotes ease and efficiency of motion for your activities. Feel how your body moves without tension. Discover how to use just the right amount of muscular effort in the correct places to produce flowing movement for yoga, Pilates, fitness, sports, dance, or life. Fluidity, power, and grace can't be achieved when the muscles are gripping and tightening. They have to activate, engage, and lengthen. Chakra Rocking Massage speeds up the recuperation time between exercise sessions or when you are not feeling well. Clearing the body of unwanted muscular tension gives you more energy for better balance, vitality, longevity, and quality of life.

# Practicing the Rocking Motion for the Seven Chakra Rocking Massage Exercises

**Y**oga teaches that your breath, or "life force," runs through each of your "energy centers," or chakras. The most important element of the Chakra Rocking Massage is deep relaxation breathing. This aids in muscle relaxation and the fluid rocking motion. If you hold your breath or breathe shallowly, the muscles tighten. Deep relaxation breathing involves long, slow, even inhalations and exhalations. Breathe in and out through your nose and mouth.

## Safety

Those with spine issues should review the execution of the Seven Chakra Rocking Massage Exercises and motions with a medical professional for any necessary modifications or contraindications.

### Preparation for Practicing the Chakra Rocking Massage Motion

This time is just for you. Avoid outside distractions as you prepare for the Rocking Massage.

- You may want to play soft music or light a candle. You will need a slightly cushioned mat, a blanket, or a towel. A carpeted surface may be more comfortable. A yoga sticky mat will not work. Your body cannot slide along it. It may be necessary to elevate your head. Place a folded towel under your head. Keep the towel flat. The back of your head needs to gently slide during the rocking motion.

- Use the rocking motion for each of the seven Chakra Rocking Massage Exercises in chapter five. There are different body positions for the exercises. Spend a few minutes with each exercise.

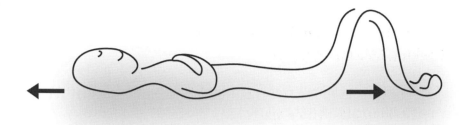

## Starting Position for Practicing the Chakra Rocking Massage Motion

Lie on your back with knees bent, feet flat on the floor, and legs hip-width apart; rest your arms across your chest. Your heels should be about 12 inches away from your buttocks. The motion should be a continuous, slow, rhythmic action. The body rocks backward and then automatically rolls forward in response. The rhythm seamlessly repeats itself without pausing. Breathe slowly and smoothly.

## Practice the Chakra Rocking Massage Motion

- Keep your feet in place and initiate the rock-and-roll motion of your body with a gentle push of your feet against the floor. The motion starts from the heels and reverberates into your pelvic floor. The name for this is the "heel/sit-bone connection." Your sit bones are the bones located at the base of your pelvis. (You can feel them when you rock side to side in a sitting position.)

- Rock your entire body as a unit, without pausing, in a sliding motion back and forth along the floor. The weight shift takes place within a tiny range of motion; your body moves approximately one to two inches backward and one to two inches forward. The rocking rhythm is smooth and continuous.

- Keep your lower back and abdominal area relaxed. Your lower back should not press against the floor, as that would tighten your lower back, which is the opposite of your intention. The gentle rocking motion lengthens the lower back when the body moves backward and it naturally arches your back when the body slides forward. Your back muscles will gradually relax because of the rocking massage motion.

- Relax your neck, your jaw, and the area directly behind your ears. The head will gently slide. Your chin moves up and down as a natural reaction to the slight push from your feet.

- Drape your arms across your body. Relax your arm and hand muscles. Feel the weight of your arms as they give in to gravity's downward pull. You are in the "zone" when the back of your shoulder girdle and head slide along the floor. You may find it more comfortable to rest your arms by your sides.

- Maintain a fluid rocking motion with no stops and starts. Visualize a slow, continuous, rhythmic rocking motion of the entire body. Try not to use too much effort to push back from your feet. Let go and enjoy the natural forward and backward rocking rhythm. Consciously relax and feel your muscles go limp. Allow the joints to move like gentle shock absorbers. Notice the weight of your body. Give in to gravity. Be patient. There is a tendency to grip your muscles throughout the day. It takes time to allow the muscles to become soft and supple.

- Try not to make the gentle rock happen. Allow the rocking motion to sequence freely through your whole body. Your entire body naturally knows what to do—if you relax each part.

### Helpful Tips for the Chakra Rocking Massage Motion

- The actual rocking motion is present in all movements. This is due to the rhythmical interplay between your hip flexors (iliopsoas muscles, located deep within your pelvis) and your extensor muscles (hamstrings, located at the back of your thighs). For example, every time you transition from lying down to sitting to standing, the pelvis rocks on top of the legs.

- For best results, continuously relax your body enough to allow an open conduit for an equal and opposite, backward and forward, push/pull motion through your heels/ankles. This motion travels into your sit bones, up the vertebrae, and out the top of your head. The motion then travels back down again through each segment of the body. There is a subtle lengthening of the head vertically away from the tailbone and vice versa. The names of these bone landmarks are the heel/sit bone and top of the head/tailbone connection.

- It is possible for the motion initiated by pushing from the feet to become "stuck" somewhere. For example, your shoulder blades might not be effortlessly moving and sliding along the mat. You may habitually store muscle tightness. With practice, you will dissolve this tension pattern. Relax and have fun!

# 5

# The Seven
# Chakra Rocking
# Massage Exercises

Y ou may choose to perform the rocking motion in the First Chakra Rocking Massage position for all seven of the exercises. This may be the most comfortable position for you.

Perform each of the seven self-massage exercises for approximately two to three minutes. Practice the First Chakra Rocking Massage Exercise several times until you feel comfortable. Gradually add the other six exercises. Be patient and gentle with yourself. Practice the Chakra Rocking Massage ten to fifteen minutes once a week.

The recipe cards in chapter two help you to understand the chakras. Refer to them in order to set your intention. For example, in the first exercise, picture the air you breathe as the color red. Visualize it circling around the tailbone area. The first chakra's life lesson relates to your physical needs.

Observe this aspect of your life with the gentle reassurance of a loving mother for a child. You may choose to repeat the first chakra affirmation silently, while rocking.

Practice the Chakra Rocking Massage Exercises while picturing the helpful visual imagery located after the set-up of each exercise. The imagery will aid you in focusing on the color, relaxation, and breathing.

## The Root/Base (First) Chakra Rocking Massage Exercise

**Color:** Red

**Location:** The root/base chakra; base of the spine/tailbone

**Type of Energy:** Survival instinct/quest for physical comfort

**Safety:** Those with spine issues should review the execution of the Seven Chakra Rocking Massage Exercises with a medical professional for any necessary modifications or contraindications.

**Position:** Lie on your back with knees bent, feet flat on the floor, and legs hip-width apart; rest your arms across your chest. Your heels should be about 12 inches away from your buttocks.

**Start:** Perform the Chakra Rocking Massage motion described in chapter four for several minutes. Relax and enjoy.

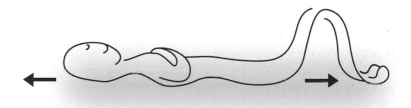

**Affirmation:** Always begin by paying attention to the rhythm of your breathing. Breathe slowly and deeply through your nose and mouth. While rocking, periodically repeat the affirmation: "I am grounded and supported in all areas of my life. I feel worthy of abundance."

## *Visual Imagery Guide—First Chakra*

The following visual images aid you in the exercise. Over time, you might develop your own visual images.

- Imagine, as you breathe in, a reddish glow fills you, penetrating every cell of your being. As you breathe, visualize a red wheel that spins around your tailbone. This is where the first chakra is located.

- Select a personal image, such as a beautiful red rose, sunset, apple, or cardinal, to focus on.

- Loosely allow your body to rock back and forth like red Jell-O.

## Sacral (Second) Chakra
## Rocking Massage Exercise

**Color:** Orange

**Location:** The sacral chakra; below the waist.

**Type of Energy:** Pleasure

**Safety:** Those with spine issues should review the execution of the Seven Chakra Rocking Massage Exercises with a medical professional for any necessary modifications or contraindications.

**Position:** As with the first chakra exercise, lie on your back with knees bent, feet flat on the floor, and legs hip-width apart; rest your arms across your chest. Your heels should be about 12 inches away from your buttocks. Drop your right knee out to your side. Your left leg stays bent, foot flat on the floor, knee facing the ceiling.

**Start:** Perform the Chakra Rocking Massage motion described in chapter four. Push from the sole of the left foot and outer edge of the right foot. Change sides by returning the right knee to its original position and drop the left knee out to your side. Perform the rocking motion for several minutes.

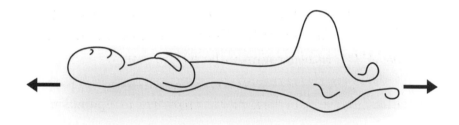

**Affirmation:** Maintain awareness of the rhythm of your breathing. Breathe slowly and deeply. Silently repeat the affirmation from time to time: "I am enjoying and appreciating the goodness of life, including my relationships."

## *Visual Imagery Guide—Second Chakra*

The following visual images aid you in the exercise. Over time, you might develop your own visual images.

- Imagine as you breathe in you are filling your body with a warm orange glow that represents vitality. Breathe in the color orange. Visualize the color moving around your hips and picture an orange kaleidoscope spinning below your navel. This is the location of the second chakra.

- Visualize a juicy orange, a bird of paradise, or a pumpkin.

- Imagine lying on a large skateboard with someone rocking you back and forth.

## Solar Plexus (Third) Chakra
## Rocking Massage Exercise

**Color:** Yellow

**Location:** The solar plexus chakra; navel

**Type of Energy:** Power

**Safety:** Those with spine issues should review the execution of the Seven Chakra Rocking Massage Exercises with a medical professional for any necessary modifications or contraindications. If you have hip limitations, after completing the exercise, ease out of the position by straightening your legs.

**Position:** As with the first chakra exercise, lie on your back with knees bent, feet flat on the floor, and legs hip-width apart; rest your arms across your chest. Your heels should be about 12 inches away from your buttocks. This time, drop both legs out to your sides. The soles of your feet are together in a frog-like position.

**Start:** Perform the Chakra Rocking Massage motion described in chapter four. Gently push from the outer edges of your feet to initiate the rocking motion and perform the motion for several minutes.

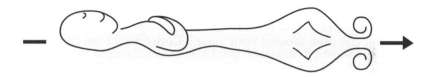

**Affirmation:** Maintain awareness of the rhythm of your breathing. Breathe slowly and deeply. Silently repeat the affirmation from time to time: "I am powerful and I am cultivating more courage. I enlist cooperation and support when needed."

arm circles. The shoulder girdle, arms, and hand muscles remain limp and tension-free. Allow gravity to help you feel the weight of your arms.

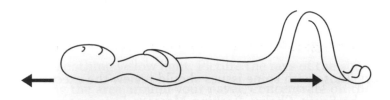

**Start:** Perform the Chakra Rocking Massage motion described in chapter four. While rocking, add arm circles, beginning with arms across your chest as you would to take off a T-shirt. Start the full circles overhead, and continue to circle your arms out to your sides and then down toward your feet. Return arms to your chest. Repeat the arm circles three to five times while continuing the rocking motion.

The next movements are like *putting on* a T-shirt. While continuing the rocking motion, you will reverse the arm circles, from bottom to top. Begin with the arms across your chest. Create large, full circles with the arms along your body, starting toward your feet. Open arms out to your sides and continue to circle, lifting them overhead. Return the arms to your chest. Repeat the arm circles three to five times while continuing the rocking motion.

**Affirmation:** Maintain awareness of your breathing rhythms, while silently repeating the affirmation: "I am unconditional love. I have faith that love is the strongest force in the universe."

## *Visual Imagery Guide—Fourth Chakra*

The following visual images aid you in the exercise. Over time, you might develop your own images.

- Imagine as you breathe in you are filling your body with green light. Picture a vibrant green spinning wheel caressing your heart. This is where the fourth chakra is located.

- Visualize green tropical plants, a forest, or a jade gemstone.

- Allow your muscles, joints, and bones to be as soft as clouds. Picture a tree gently swaying in the breeze.

## Throat (Fifth) Chakra
## Rocking Massage Exercise

**Color:** Sky Blue

**Location:** The throat chakra; neck

**Type of Energy:** Creativity/communication

**Safety:** Those with spine issues should review the execution of the Seven Chakra Rocking Massage Exercises with a medical professional for any necessary modifications or contraindications. Do not practice this chakra exercise if you have neck problems.

**Position:** As with the first chakra exercise, lie on your back with knees bent, feet flat on the floor, and legs hip-width apart; rest your arms across your chest. Your heels should be about 12 inches away from your buttocks.

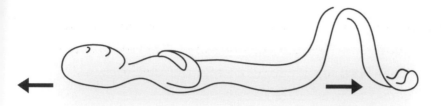

**Start**  Perform the Chakra Rocking Massage motion described in chapter four. While rocking, gently move your head. The rocking motion from your feet helps to orchestrate these slow head movements. Gradually allow your head to move to the right, then return slowly to center. While keeping your neck relaxed, move your head to the left. Repeat the rocking motion for several minutes. You may choose to repeat the head movements, too.

**Affirmation:**  Maintain awareness of your breathing rhythms while silently repeating the affirmation: "I am the inspired wisdom within you. I have the gift of a childlike curiosity for life."

### *Visual Imagery Guide—Fifth Chakra*

The following visual images aid you in the exercise. Over time, you might develop your own images.

- Imagine as you breathe in you are filling your body with a beautiful blue mist. You are wearing a necklace of swirling blue light. The fifth chakra is located around the neck.

- Visualize blue sky, the ocean, or an aquamarine stone.

- Picture the pendulum of a grandfather clock as your body swings rhythmically. Your muscles are becoming supple.

## The Third-Eye (Sixth) Chakra Rocking Massage Exercise

**Color:** Indigo

**Location:** The third-eye chakra; the space between and a little above your eyes on your forehead

**Type of Energy:** Intuition

**Safety:** Those with spine issues should review the execution of the Seven Chakra Rocking Massage Exercises with a medical professional for any necessary modifications or contraindications. Do not practice this chakra exercise if you have neck, shoulder, or hip problems.

**Position:** As with the first chakra exercise, lie on your back with knees bent, feet flat on the floor, and legs hip-width apart; rest your arms across your chest. Your heels should be about 12 inches away from your buttocks. For this exercise, you may need to bring your heels closer to your hips.

Lift your hips approximately two inches off the floor, creating a hammock-like shape with your body. The feet, middle back, upper back, and head are on the floor while you rock.

**Start**  Perform the Chakra Rocking Massage motion described in chapter four.

The rib cage, upper back, and head should slide effortlessly along the floor while you perform the rocking motion. Allow the back of your legs, hips, and back to go limp like the support of a hammock. Perform the rocking motion for several minutes. Instead of lifting the hips up and down, continue the forward and backward hip motion.

If your pelvic muscles tighten, relax back to the floor. If your hamstrings tighten, lie flat on your back. Gently draw your legs toward your chest. Slowly stretch the back of your legs and hips. Now continue with the exercise.

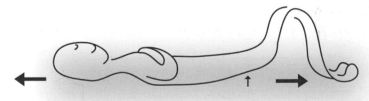

**Affirmation:** Maintain awareness of your breathing rhythms, while silently repeating, "I use my imagery and visualization. I renew my energy in nature. I am grateful for easy and effortless action. I am observing the magic of life."

### *Visual Imagery Guide—Sixth Chakra*

The following visual images aid you in the exercise. Over time, you might develop your own images.

- Imagine when you breathe in you are filling your body with indigo light. See the space in between your eyes as a spinning wheel of indigo light. Bathe your forehead in this soothing, violet-blue light. This is where the sixth chakra is located.

- Visualize an indigo night sky, a sapphire, or a butterfly.

- Picture someone gently rocking you. Relax and enjoy the ride.

## The Crown (Seventh) Chakra
## Rocking Massage Exercise

**Color:** Violet

**Location:** The crown chakra; the top of your head

**Type of Energy:** Spiritual

**Safety:** Those with spine issues should review the execution of the Seven Chakra Rocking Massage Exercises with a medical professional for any necessary modifications or contraindications. Do not practice this chakra exercise if you have hip problems.

**Position:** As with the first chakra exercise, lie on your back with knees bent, feet flat on the floor, and legs hip-width apart; rest your arms across your chest. Your heels should be about 12 inches away from your buttocks. Now drop both knees out to the side like a frog, soles of your feet together.

This exercise challenges your coordination because your entire body circles while rocking forward and back.

Begin the rocking motion. Add clockwise circles. Your goal is to rock AND circle the entire body. For example, first check whether your hips are circling. Next, check your rib cage, then your shoulder girdle, and finally your head. Maintain a continuous fluid rhythm. Over time, this motion will become second nature.

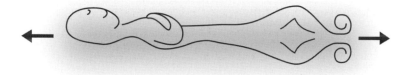

**Start:** Begin the Chakra Rocking Massage motion described in chapter four. Gently push from the outer edges of your feet to produce the rocking motion. Once your body feels comfortable, add a clockwise circling motion to your entire body. Your legs, hips, ribs, shoulder girdle, and head are all circling. Imagine your entire body is lying on a revolving disc. Perform the rocking and circling motion for several minutes.

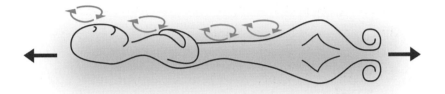

Now you'll reverse the motion. Circle in a counter-clockwise direction. Perform the rocking and circling motion for several minutes.

**Affirmation:** Maintain awareness of your breathing rhythms, while silently repeating the affirmation: "I am at peace. I am compassionate and enjoy helping others."

### Visual Imagery Guide—Seventh Chakra

The following visual images aid you in the exercise. Over time, you might develop your own images.

- Imagine when you breathe in you are filling your body with violet light. Picture a spinning wheel of violet light at the top of your head and allow the light to pour into your body and fill you with peace. The seventh chakra is located at the top of your head.

- Visualize a purple amethyst, a plum, or violets.

- The muscles take on lengthening and widening characteristics. Feel your trunk muscles become malleable; feel your back muscles spread like pancake batter across a pan.

- Relax your back muscles until they feel like JELL-O. Picture molded JELL-O rocking forward and back and wobbling in circles.

By performing the Seven Chakra Rocking Massage Exercises, you have harmonized your seven energy centers as you would tune a fine musical instrument. Your ultimate goal is to perform all seven exercises by seamlessly moving from one to the next until you have completed them. It only takes about 15 minutes.

# Three-Dimensional
# Balloon Breathing
# Using Chakra Colors

**B**reathing is the only involuntary system of the body that we can consciously control. Visual imagery–based breathing techniques are the key to radiant health. The images combine with the breathing to link to the mind/body connection. Breathing is the bridge between the mind, body, and spirit. We take between 16,000 and 23,000 breaths per day, yet we rarely stop to take a deep, focused breath. No wonder we feel stressed throughout our day.

The breathing exercises in this book harness a dormant power system within your body. Tap into the images in these breathing exercises anytime, anywhere—no one around you will know you are practicing efficient breathing! This helps you live a life filled with vitality and peace.

Many of us breathe shallowly. The common name for it is "shallow chest breathing." We barely fill the upper area of the chest with our inhalations, sometimes only inhaling about one-third of the oxygen needed by the lungs. We stop filling the belly with air even though the breathing mechanism allows for it. This is evident in the unrestricted movements of a baby's belly.

Shallow breathing weakens the diaphragm muscle and the muscles of the ribs. It deprives the chest and abdominal area of stimulation, which affects digestion and circulation. Stale air remains lodged in the lower lungs. The blood lacks the necessary oxygen, leading to a buildup of toxins. Deep relaxation breathing promotes calmness, confidence, vitality, and harmony within your life. In this chapter, you will learn several relaxation-breathing techniques.

## Benefits of Daily Deep Relaxation Breathing Breaks

There are many benefits to deep relaxation breathing techniques.

- The Vertical, Horizontal, Sagittal, and Three-Dimensional Balloon Breathing techniques are mainly practical. For a quick and convenient pick-me-up, use them during a hectic workday or on a long plane flight. No fancy equipment is necessary to energize and/or relax your body; just use your breathing. Practice your breathing in the morning, before sleep, or even while standing in a long line. Proper breathing is essential for stretching, yoga, rehabilitation, sports, fitness, dance, Pilates, and martial arts as an excellent warm-up and cool-down.

- These breathing techniques provide a physical sense of security, confidence, grounding, vitality, and passion for being alive. The chakra color imagery enhances these feelings. Visualize the colors to take in more volumes of air. For example, imagine the air around you is a rich, deep red. As you breathe in, your whole body fills with red energy.

- The Three-Dimensional Breathing provides inner support for your posture and assists with the Chakra Rocking Massage Exercises, helping you to relax tight muscles along the spine, neck, shoulders, rib cage, and lower back (chapter five).

- Efficient breathing directly relates to calming the nervous system, which enhances your ability to cope with stress. Breathing is the link to our state of mind. Fear shortens our breathing. The consequence of stress makes your breathing so shallow that it resides high in the chest. Breathing becomes erratic when we feel anxious. It practically disappears when we concentrate hard. Breath training eradicates the breakdown of the physical body due to stress.

- By making more room for air in the body, Three-Dimensional Balloon Breathing pushes out and filters stagnant air. These breathing techniques invigorate the muscles of the ribs, diaphragm, and back. This efficient diaphragmatic breathing is an inner massage that replenishes your organs and increases lung capacity. Exercising your respiratory system improves metabolic and cardiovascular function.

- Visual imagery–based breathing exercises develop your powers of paying attention to your breathing, which is your immediate life-sustaining source. You can affect those powers. This is breath "insurance" for better concentration, energy levels, sleep patterns, and digestion. You can reach the peaceful breathing rhythm of meditation through practice.

- For singers, actors, teachers, and speakers, these deep diaphragmatic breathing exercises are excellent for the warm-up, range, projection, and care of the voice. It adds authority and calmness to the voice.

- The breathing techniques quiet the mind for the Creative Chakra Color Meditation by providing concrete visual pictures (see chapter eight).

## Anatomy Lesson—See the Diaphragm Muscle, Feel it, Transform your Health

You can maximize your breathing mechanism by thoroughly understanding how it works. The diaphragm is the largest muscle in the body. It connects to the breastbone, the lower ribs, and the lower spine. It serves as a floor for the chest and a ceiling for the stomach. It has a parachute shape.

During an efficient inhalation, the diaphragm drops down toward the abdomen. In order for the diaphragm to work properly, the abdominal muscles must relax. If not, the diaphragm cannot drop down. You must inhale plenty of air to accomplish a deep diaphragmatic breath. Shallow breathing allows air only into the narrower passages of the chest. This is where the term *shallow chest breathing* comes from. Shallow breathing is a big contributor to lethargy, anxiety, and stress in our lives.

During efficient exhalation, the diaphragm will relax and move up into the chest. The motion executed by a gentle tightening of the abdominal wall relaxes the chest as the ribs press toward the lungs.

## Helpful Tips for Three-Dimensional Balloon Breathing

- To enhance your mind/body connection, add chakra color imagery to your Vertical, Horizontal, Sagittal, and Three-Dimensional Balloon Breathing exercises. When you inhale, visualize filling your body with the color red, orange, yellow, green, blue, indigo, or violet. The colors help you to take slow, long, and even inhalations and exhalations.

- Perform these breathing exercises daily, in any position— sitting, standing, lying down, or walking. You can do them anytime, anywhere.

- Relax all the muscles of your body. Maintain good posture. Turn your focus inward and pay attention to your breathing. Exclude everything else in your life.

## Tips for Breathing Safety and Success

● Practice for only three to five minutes a session. Discontinue practice at any sign of strain, tension, or light-headedness. Working with your breathing takes time, patience, and concentration. Never hold your breath during the breathing techniques.

● Imagine you are trickling air in and out very slowly through a drinking straw. These are slow, even, deep, and tranquil breaths. Initially, you may choose to use an actual straw to help practice.

● In yoga, it is more relaxing to breathe in through the nose and out through the nose. The nose filters impurities in the air; however, in Three-Dimensional Breathing, allow the air to come in and out slowly through your nose and mouth. This is especially helpful for people with allergies or asthma.

● Allow your breath to flow naturally without force or strain. Find a rhythm comfortable for you. Balance the length of your inhalations and exhalations. You may choose to use the second hand on a watch. Initially, this may be about a slow, eight-second inhalation and a slow, eight-second exhalation. Practice over time and you may gradually increase this rhythm to a comfortable twenty-second inhalation, and a twenty-second exhalation. The imaginary straw is the key to taking in more air and discovering spaces to put the air. This may take some time. Chronic tension in the muscles must gradually relax.

## Position for Balloon Breathing

Remember, you can practice the relaxation breathing in this chapter in any position—standing, sitting, lying down, or even during a slow walk. The following Constructive Rest Pose is an ideal way to begin your breathing practice. You can relax more readily in this position. Wear loose, comfortable clothing. Elevate your head slightly with a towel. This lengthens your neck. Tip your chin toward your chest. Your air passages become open for a free exchange of oxygen.

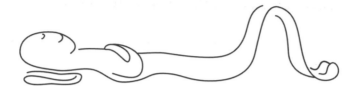

- Lie on your back with your knees bent. The soles of your feet are on the floor, approximately two feet apart.

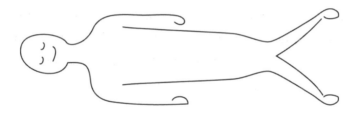

- Allow your knees to meet, creating a teepee shape with your legs. Your bent knees encourage your lower back to relax.

- Your arms are by your sides. Keep your shoulders down, away from your ears.

## The Vertical Balloon Breathing Exercise

Maintain good posture, relax, and focus within on your breathing.

### *Visual Imagery Guide—Vertical Balloon Breathing*

Start:

- Start by practicing several breaths. Visualize directing your intake of air up and down, like filling up a colorful sausage-shaped balloon. Exhale while picturing the balloon shrinking. Repeat several times.

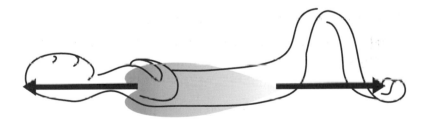

- Picture a long, heart-shaped balloon inside your body. Visualize filling this balloon vertically with air, up and down. The balloon lengthens and expands with your long, slow inhalations and shrinks on your exhalations. Repeat several times.

- Inhale: Imagine the balloon simultaneously expanding from the bottom of your hips to the top of your shoulders with your inhalations. Exhale: Visualize the balloon deflating into the center of your body.

- Inhale: Picture a colorful balloon as it expands along your spine. Imagine you are getting taller. Sense your tailbone area lengthening. In your mind's eye, visualize the head rising like a helium balloon. Exhale.

- Place one hand high on your chest and the other hand low on your belly. If you inhale very slowly through an imaginary straw, you will feel your hands stretch away from each other. Exhale: Notice how your hands automatically come together.

- Ask yourself a few questions to enhance body awareness. Inhale: Did you feel your rib cage rise up away from your hips on your inhalations? Fill the entire back surfaces of your body with air; lower back, rib cage, and shoulder blades. Does your spine feel longer? Did you feel your hips and shoulders stretch away from one another? Exhale: Did you feel the muscles along the spine relax? Ask these questions while you inhale and exhale to ensure you have the correct results. Repeat several times.

## Horizontal Balloon Breathing Exercise

Relax and align your body. Notice your breathing.

*Visual Imagery Guide—Horizontal Balloon Breathing*

Start:

- Start by practicing several breaths. Direct the air side-to-side while visualizing a heart-shaped balloon growing wider within your chest, ribs, and belly. Exhale while picturing the balloon shrinking. Repeat several times.

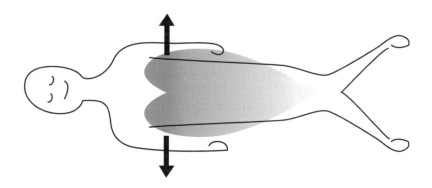

- Place your hands on either side of your rib cage with your fingertips touching. Inhale: If you breathe slowly through an imaginary straw, your fingertips will move several inches away from one another. Exhale: Your hands gradually come back together. Repeat several times.

- Repeat the Horizontal Balloon Breathing with your hands on your belly several times. Visualize a colorful, wide balloon. Inhale and feel your fingertips move away from one another. Exhale and feel your hands come back together. This is like the slow motion of a fireplace bellows opening and closing. Repeat several times.

- These are long, slow, and even inhalations and exhalations. Keep it gentle. Picture the balloon about to pop before you let the air out.

## Sagittal Balloon Breathing Exercise

Relax and align your body. Pay attention to what's going on within your body by noticing your breathing.

### Visual Imagery Guide—Sagittal Balloon Breathing

Start:

- Start by practicing several breaths. Visualize filling a colorful, fat balloon with air. Direct the air forward and backward, allowing your body to feel thick. Exhale: Picture the balloon slowly deflating. Repeat several times.

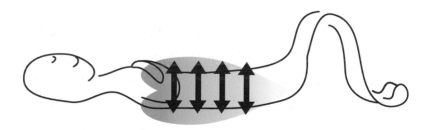

- Place one hand on your belly and your other hand beneath your lower back. Picture a thick, fat, heart-shaped balloon inside your body. Inhale: Visualize filling this balloon forward and backward. This makes your body feel thick. Feel your hand rise toward the ceiling while the other hand presses into the floor. Exhale. Repeat several times.

- Inhale: Feel a colorful balloon thicken as it simultaneously expands toward the ceiling and into the floor. Exhale: Visualize the balloon flattening or deflating within your body. It's like letting the air out of a blow-up mattress. Feel the weight of your body sink into the floor as you exhale. Repeat several times.

- Increase your body awareness by asking yourself a few questions. During your inhalations, did you feel your chest, rib cage, and belly stretch up to the ceiling? Did you simultaneously feel the back surfaces of your body expand into the floor around your shoulder blades, rib cage, and lower back area?

## Three-Dimensional Balloon Breathing Exercise

You may choose to warm up for the Three-Dimensional Balloon Breathing with the Vertical, Horizontal, and Sagittal Balloon Breathing Exercises.

### *Visual Imagery Guide—Three-Dimensional Balloon Breathing*

Start:

- Start by practicing several breaths. Visualize a colorful balloon filling with air. During the first part of the inhalation, picture a sausage-shaped balloon, which then becomes a wide balloon, and finally a fat balloon. Direct the air up and down, sideways, and forward and back, making your body feel tall, wide, and thick. Exhale. Repeat several times.

- Picture a long, wide, and thick heart-shaped balloon inside your body. Visualize filling this balloon with air vertically

(up and down), horizontally (side to side), and sagittally (forward and backward). This is happening during each single inhalation. Try this several times.

- Inhale: Feel your body stretch and open from the inside outward. Your balloon has length, width, and depth. Exhale: Picture the balloon shrinking from all three directions. Your balloon deflates into the center of your body. Take several long, slow, and tranquil breaths.

- Inhale: Envision inflating a huge, colorful balloon within your body. Exhale: Picture the balloon collapsing or deflating.

- Mix up the directions of your single inhalation between length, width, and depth. Clearly picture each separate direction in your mind. As you practice each single inhalation, say, "up and down," "side-to-side," and finally, "forward and backward." Exhale.

Practice these breathing exercises several times a day for stress management and an improved state of well-being. Remember, the exercises can be done anytime and anywhere, while sitting, standing, lying down, and walking. Consider your breathing exercises a healthy habit as important as brushing your teeth.

After your breathing exercises, pay attention to how you feel. Your muscles are deeply relaxed. Your mind is quiet. You feel calm. Through regular practice, you will notice improvements in your concentration and energy level.

You will have better posture because you are more aware of the vertical, horizontal, and sagittal space within and around your body. We can move in all three planes through space. You can move primarily in the vertical direction (up and down), like a basketball lay-up or dunk, or a volleyball dig or spike. You can move in the horizontal direction (side to side), like a hockey goalie laterally moving to protect the space in front of the net. You can move in the sagittal direction (forward and backward), like a boxer.

Our bodies also have (vertical) length, (horizontal) width, and (sagittal) depth. The Three-Dimensional Balloon Breathing makes it possible to direct your inhalations into one or all three of these very distinct regions within the body. Through Three-Dimensional Balloon Breathing, you will feel what it is like to fill the interior spaces of your body with air up and down, side to side, and forward and back.

# 7

## Progressive Relaxation Using the Chakra Colors

**P**rogressive Relaxation is a body-awareness technique that teaches you how to relax your muscles. As tension builds up in our muscles over the years, the natural flow of energy within our bodies is blocked. The system in this book keeps this vital energy flowing freely to maintain good health.

Practice Progressive Relaxation alone, before, or after your Chakra Rocking Massage Exercises (chapter five). Perform it lying down or in a sitting position, such as in your office chair. Dedicate a few minutes each day to unwind and let go. By practicing the art of Progressive Relaxation, you can manage daily stress and sleep problems and lessen the effects when you feel under the weather. Accomplish this by learning to become more familiar with the various muscles of your body.

## Safety

Throughout Progressive Relaxation, remember to keep your breathing even and relaxed. Hold the muscular contraction for only five seconds and feel your muscles engage, not grip.

## How to Perform Progressive Relaxation

- First tighten or contract muscles, beginning with your feet, then completely relax. You will be tightening the muscle without actually moving through space. Slowly contract then relax each muscle, moving up from your feet toward your head.

- Picture the chakra colors while you contract and relax your muscles. This helps you pinpoint tight muscles and learn to relax them. Remember to keep your breathing deep, slow, even, and tranquil. You can practice Progressive Relaxation while in a sitting position. It is even more relaxing performed while lying on your back.

## Position for Progressive Relaxation

- Lie on your back with your legs straight.

- Place arms by your side with palms facing the ceiling.

- If needed, place a pillow beneath your knees to support your lower back. For more comfort, you might also place a towel under your head.

## Preparation for Progressive Relaxation

- Rub your hands together briskly for a few seconds.

- Close your eyes and place your hands over your eyelids while imagining your eyelids becoming heavy.

- Rest your arms by your sides.

## Start Progressive Relaxation

There are seven steps in the Progressive Relaxation exercise, one for each of the seven chakras. You will visualize each of the chakra colors as you perform the exercise.

### Step One: Red

Begin by tensing your feet. Curl your toes and contract the arches of your feet. At the same time, tighten the muscles of your legs. Visualize a beautiful red light swirling around your feet and legs as you contract the muscles. Then, completely relax the muscles of your feet and legs.

### Step Two: Orange

Next, tense the hip muscles. Picture the color orange while you squeeze your buttocks muscles together. Then, spend some time allowing the hip area to become relaxed.

### Step Three: Yellow

Continue with the stomach. Tighten up your abdominal muscles by sinking your navel toward your spine. Visualize the warm yellow rays of the sun spiraling around your navel. Relax . . .

### Step Four: Green

Picture the color green while you tighten your chest area and squeeze your shoulder blades together by contracting your upper back muscles. Relax . . .

### Step Five: Blue

Contract the muscles of your neck, arms, and hands. Make fists with your hands. Picture a beautiful sky-blue necklace of light. Then completely relax . . .

### Step Six: Indigo

Crinkle up the muscles of your face. Furrow your brow. Visualize the color indigo. Then relax your face and let go of all your thoughts.

### Step Seven: Violet

Open your eyes and mouth wide and close them tight. Picture the color violet. Then relax.

Allow yourself to go deeper and deeper into total body relaxation. Imagine you are floating in a colorful dream. Picture yourself lying on a supportive down comforter. "Give in" to gravity's downward pull. Feel your body getting heavier and heavier, sinking into the floor. Spend time enjoying this new state of deep relaxation!

8

# Creative Chakra
# Color Meditation

**P**erform the Creative Chakra Color Meditation in any position, anytime, anywhere. Meditation provides many benefits to the mind, body, and spirit. These benefits include stress relief, mental acuity, relaxation, lower blood pressure, and increased energy.

Meditation is a low-tech antidote to stress. Instead of sitting in front of the computer or TV screen, use meditation to quiet the mind. The easiest position for meditation is to sit straight or lie down. Focus on your breathing.

## Tips for Creative Chakra Color Meditation

Put your attention on the Vertical, Horizontal, Sagittal, or Three-Dimensional Balloon Breathing techniques outlined in chapter six. Many of us have a hard time meditating. These new visual imagery-based breathing techniques provide you with a tangible and easy-to-understand path to successful meditation. While you focus on your breathing, you block negative thoughts and open the gateway to a quiet, still mind. These are slow, long, even, and tranquil breaths. You may choose to breathe through the mouth and nose.

- Creative Chakra Color Meditation provides a method to replace negative thought patterns with positive feelings of self-esteem. Every creation begins with an idea, a plan, or a blueprint. Don't let obsolete blueprints define who you are. Redesign, upgrade, and modernize your thoughts through Creative Chakra Color Meditation. Imagine that the inhaling breath brings with it one of the following traits: security, creativity, confidence, love, gratitude, kindness, or serenity. Silently repeat the selected "trait" word during the exhaling breath. Spend five to ten minutes inhaling, imagining, and exhaling. If your mind wanders, come back to your breathing.

- Visualize your intake of air as a soothing color. Meditation using color has a profound impact on calming your nervous system. Imbue or instill each trait with the following chakra colors:

  **Red:** Stability, security
  **Orange:** Creativity
  **Yellow:** Confidence, strength
  **Green:** Love
  **Blue:** Gratitude
  **Indigo:** Kindness
  **Violet:** Joy, peace

- Spend as much time as you like in meditation.

# 9

# Stretching Using
# Chakra Colors

I n our society, even the simplest movements are often rushed and constricted. A stretching routine can benefit you in several ways.

- Slow stretching calms your nervous system and provides a sense of vitality. Your muscles relax more during the Chakra Rocking Massage Exercises through these stretches (see chapter five).

- Stretching also enhances the body's blood and nutrient supply. Tense muscles are more toxic and can cause lethargy. Stretching increases the quantity of synovial fluid within our joints, maintaining their health. Stretching pinpoints tight muscles and relieves lower back discomfort.

- Last, stretching is one of the keys to feeling young. Children are always in motion, constantly stretching their bodies into different positions. As adults, we can strive to do the same thing. A routine stretching program is an important fitness component for a healthy adult. Stretching will help the muscles and connective tissue stay elongated and elastic and improve circulation, concentration, and digestion, as well as sleep patterns. Tense muscles contribute to stress. Supple muscles create deep relaxation.

For each exercise, you will choose an affirmation, use the Three-Dimensional Balloon Breathing technique (chapter six), and pick a chakra color to focus on.

## Affirmation

Select one of the following seven chakra-related affirmations and silently repeat it while holding a stretch.

"I am secure in all areas of my life."

"I am enjoying and appreciating the goodness of life, including my relationships."

"I enlist cooperation and support when needed."

"I am unconditional love."

"I have the gift of a childlike curiosity for life."

"I am grateful for easy and effortless action."

"I am at peace."

## Breathing

Increase your muscle relaxation during each of your stretches by using Three-Dimensional Balloon Breathing, as discussed in chapter six.

## *Stretching*

While you stretch, breathe in any of the seven chakra colors you choose. Breathe in the color red, orange, yellow, green, blue, indigo, or violet. Breathe out and visualize all the tension leaving your body.

### Preparation for Your Stretching Program

- Find a space large enough for your body to stretch out fully in all directions.

- For cushioning, use a mat or blanket, or place a towel on a carpet.

- Elevate your head slightly, for more comfort, with a small pillow or extra towel.

- This is your personal time without any outside distractions. Using light music may enhance your relaxation.

## Safety

A static stretch is a stretch that you hold that triggers the "stretch reflex." As you stay in a stretch position, the muscles relax a bit more. Hold each stretch for a minimum of thirty seconds and up to a minute. Stretch to the point of "comfortable tension," never pain. In any movement, if it feels bad, it is. Stretching too far may cause soreness. Move slowly and smoothly into and out of your stretches. Try to relax your entire body during a stretch. You may decide to stretch before an activity, but first warm up with a five-minute walk.

## Basic Hamstring and Hip Stretch

Picture breathing in beautiful colors and consciously relax the tension-filled areas.

### *Position:*

- Lie flat on your back on the floor with your right support leg bent and the sole of the foot on the floor.

- Raise your left leg with your knee pointing to the ceiling.

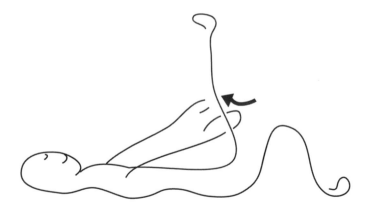

- Bring your left thigh to your chest. Place your hands behind your left leg to assist.

### Start: Use Affirmations, Breathing, and Chakra Colors

- Slowly extend your left leg. Keep it slightly bent to avoid straining your hamstrings. Flex your foot to add a calf stretch. Keep your bottom on the floor. Check that your spine is in "neutral" and elongate the back and neck.

- Gently lower the leg to release the stretch.

- Repeat the stretch with the other leg.

### Hamstring and Inner Thigh Stretch

The key to letting go in a stretch is paying attention to your breathing.

*Position:*

● Lie flat on your back with your right support leg bent. The sole of the foot is on the floor.

● Raise your left leg.

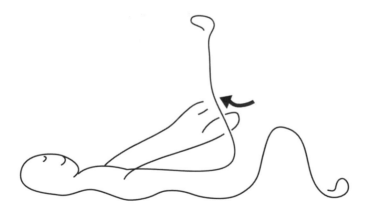

- Place your hands at the back of the left leg for assistance and move it out to the side of your body. It is now in an externally rotated position.

*Start:*

- Slowly extend your left leg, but keep it slightly bent. Flex your foot to add a calf stretch. Keep your bottom on the floor. Check that your spine is in "neutral." Elongate the back and neck.

- Now, repeat the stretch with the other leg.

## Hamstring and Outer Thigh Stretch

Pay attention to the tight areas. Breathe and visualize the tension dissipating.

*Safety:*

Omit this exercise if you have had a hip replacement. Practice the Basic Hamstring and Hip Stretch with the permission of your medical professional.

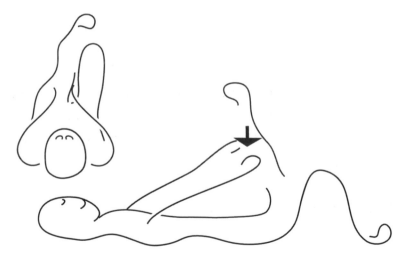

## Position:

- Lie flat on your back with your right support leg bent and the sole of the foot on the floor.

- Raise your left leg.

- Use your hands at the back of your left leg to move your thigh across your body, toward your right side. It is now in an internally rotated position.

## Start:

- Slowly extend your left leg. Keep it slightly bent. Hug your leg toward your body and flex your foot to add a calf stretch. Check that the spine is in "neutral" and elongate the back and neck.

- Now, repeat the stretch with the other leg.

## Buttocks and Lower Back Stretch

The key to muscle relaxation is to focus on taking long, slow breaths.

*Safety:*

Omit this exercise if you have had a hip replacement. Practice the Basic Hamstring and Hip Stretch with the permission of your medical professional.

*Position:*

- Lie on your back with feet flat on the floor.

- Raise your left leg with your left ankle placed across your right knee.

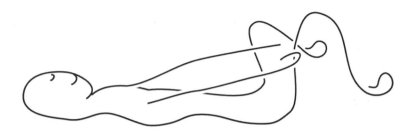

*Start:*

- Bring both feet off the floor.

- Place your hands behind the right leg.

- Draw both legs to your chest.

- Keep the pelvis on the floor. Check that your spine is in "neutral" and elongate the back and neck.

- Repeat the stretch with the other leg.

# 10

# The Core Abdominal Foundation Formula Using Chakra Colors

The Foundation Formula is the key to achieving strong abdominal muscles. It consists of very specific, anatomy-based visual images that you picture with your mind's eye. The Foundation Formula and visual imagery provide a shortcut to feeling deep, powerful contractions of your abdominal muscles toward your spine.

## Benefits of the Foundation Formula

There are many health and wellness benefits to practicing the Foundation Formula.

- Your core involves your trunk muscles: the abdominal, back, buttock, and pelvic floor muscles. Building a strong core foundation is important for everything, including your own body. Persistent practice of the Foundation Formula provides a consistent reminder to activate your deep abdominals to help you conquer unexpected physical tasks with confidence. It provides stability and mobility for lifting heavy objects. A strong center or core allows your spine to decompress.

- The Foundation Formula is practical because it can be performed anywhere. It must remain the focus to become your own traveling abdominal trainer. Practice it while at the office and during errands and chores. Perform it anywhere while in any position to strengthen the power of your core. Try it lying down, sitting, standing, walking, running, and traveling. Manage stress by using it during regular computer breaks or waiting in long lines. It is beneficial to use it in conjunction with your other routines, and it is essential for safety in any fitness regimen, Pilates routine, dance, martial art, sport, or physical therapy.

- The Foundation Formula provides an internal massage for the organs that lie behind your abdominal wall. Therefore, this life-enhancing tool improves your digestion and circulation and elevates your energy level, resulting in a positive boost to the immune system. The Foundation Formula increases the inner core body temperature, in turn producing more white blood cells, which are responsible for fighting infection. This enhances the body's resistance to colds and the flu.

- The Foundation Formula will help you become more aware of center-driven movements. Movements initiated from your core help you develop physical balance. We usually move from our limbs, which causes wear and tear on the body. The entire core operates as a shock absorber by drawing the weight of the body up away from gravity. This protects the lower extremities. The core abdominal Foundation Formula is the key to habitually initiating movements from this proper biomechanical source of support to protect your limbs and spine.

- Core trunk stabilizers involve the smaller, deeper functional muscles that are closer to the bones. Their role is to improve coordination by stabilizing the skeletal system and aligning the body. The larger structural trunk muscles are the superficial muscles just beneath the skin. They provide power for moving the body through space.

Yoga methodology teaches that the center is the place where we connect to the energies of the universe. This opens the door to trusting your gut instincts and intuition. From this place of relaxed alertness, you feel physical, mental, emotional, and spiritual harmony. A healthy core provides overall radiant well-being.

● The physical benefits to habitually using your core are stronger muscles, a trim waist, a healthier back, organ health, stress management, and spine stability.

### Analyze, Stabilize, Energize with the Foundation Formula

Use these tips to help you perform the Foundation Formula.

## Analyze

The Foundation Formula requires profound, inwardly directed focus. Practice putting your mind on the path and inward direction of the abdominal muscular contraction. The visual images and arrows allow you to do that. Without any distractions, use the corresponding visual image. Picture the anatomy of the abdominal muscles in conjunction with your focused breathing. Visualize the corresponding color to feel the strong, elastic sensation of your abdominals intertwining across each other. Say to yourself, "Wrap the muscles tighter and tighter." You will tone your stomach area as never before.

## Stabilize

You will be moving your body from the proper source of support—your center abdominal area.

*Energize*

In addition to benefiting all the systems of your body, a strong abdominal core provides limitless reserves of power for any activity. Your goal is to use this exercise throughout your day. Make it a daily habit, like brushing your teeth.

## Breathing for the Five Steps of the Foundation Formula

The type of breathing used to contract the abdominals is different from the deep-relaxation, Three-Dimensional Balloon Breathing in chapter six. Some points to keep in mind:

The key is to keep your abdominals tight between the five steps of the Foundation Formula. Never relax them.

- Inhale while KEEPING the abdominals contracted.

- Then continue inwardly shaping them on the exhalations. Upon each exhalation, powerfully contract the abdominals—deeper and deeper, tighter and tighter. You are not sucking the abdominals in. The muscle fibers are powerfully weaving across each other while deepening toward your spine. Your job is to picture this with the help of the visual images and your breath.

## *On the inhalation:*

Picture your intake of air passing through a very large imaginary straw. Visualize directing your intake of air along the entire BACK surfaces of your body, especially expanding the lower rib cage area. There should be NO expansion to the FRONT of the body during the inhalation. Your goal is to maintain the powerful abdominal contraction along the FRONT surface of the body. It may take practice, but your aim is to contract the abdominal muscles so air doesn't enter the belly. Stay focused by saying to yourself, "Keep my abdominal muscles engaged." In summary, allow the BACK of the rib cage to expand on the inhalations and maintain the abdominal contraction within the FRONT of the body.

*On the exhalation:*

Exhale forcefully, as if blowing through a trumpet! Make a powerful, deep resonating breath sound. Lengthen the sound of your exhalation and purse your lips. This is the key to powerfully contracting the deep abdominal muscles.

Coach yourself by reinforcing the following:

- Exhale through pursed lips, elongating the outward breath sound as the air powerfully releases. Whoosh...! This feels like blowing up a balloon.

- Each time you hear the exhalation, it is your reminder to contract the abdominals further inward. This breath pattern is the only way to engage the deepest layer of the stomach muscles.

- Feel the power of your breathing and your abdominals working in concert with each other. The focus is on the long, powerful diaphragmatic breath sound for every repetition.

- Exhale. Contract your abdominals by wrapping, deepening, and tightening them more and more. Say to yourself, "Wrap the abdominals."

- You can't relax the muscles during your inhalations. Say to yourself, "Keep them tight."

## Anatomy Lesson—Visualize the Four Abdominal Muscle Groups, Feel Them, Transform Your Core

The abdominal muscles consist of four layers of powerful elastic bands. These muscle fibers crisscross to form an anatomical girdle. They lie across one another at various angles. The abdominal muscles attach to your rib cage and to your pelvis and provide trunk stability and mobility.

The abdominal muscles contract as a unit to produce movements. Instead of exercising abdominal muscles as a unit, the Foundation Formula "step-by-step" process utilizes anatomy-based visual imagery to *isolate* each of the four layers of your abdominal muscle groups. This is the key to feeling your full core potential while engaging your deep abdominals. Remember, you *don't* relax the muscles between the steps.

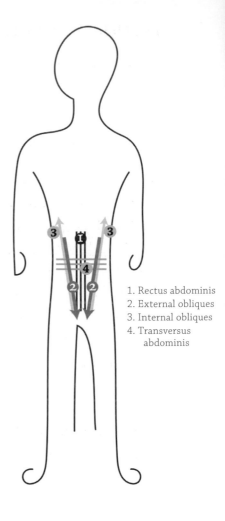

1. Rectus abdominis
2. External obliques
3. Internal obliques
4. Transversus abdominis

## The Abdominal Muscles

The following describes the abdominal muscles from the outermost layer to the deepest layer within the body.

### *Outermost Layer: Rectus Abdominis*

The outermost, rectus abdominis muscle fibers run vertically down the entire front of your body. When you see a body builder's "six-pack," you are looking at these muscles. This outer layer of the abdominals draws the ribs and hips together like a clamshell clamping shut—deep within the trunk. Try the following exercise several times to contract the abdominals deeper and deeper.

- Inhale to prepare by directing air into the back of your ribs.

- Exhale powerfully to assist the abdominal contraction. It is during the entire length of the exhalation that you draw the abdominals together like a clam clamping shut.

### *The Second Layer: External Obliques*

The external obliques are the second layer. They crisscross diagonally with the internal obliques, like an "X" that wraps around the body. These muscles compress the abdomen together and backward toward the spine. They wrap from the back of the ribs around to the front and then downward toward the hips. They cinch the body together like an extremely tight life jacket. Try this exercise several times in a row.

- Inhale.

- Exhale with a powerful breath sound while cinching your abdominals together. This feels like the strings of a life jacket drawn together with force.

## *The Third Layer: Internal Obliques*

The internal obliques are the third layer of your abdominals. These muscle fibers cross the midriff in diagonal slants from the top of the hips, upward to the lowest part of the rib cage. The powerful elastic action of these muscles feels like a zipper drawing your abdominal wall upward and backward. Try several repetitions of this exercise in a row.

- Inhale.

- Exhale while zippering your abdominals in and back toward your spine.

## *The Fourth Layer: Transversus Abdominis*

The transversus abdominis is the fourth and deepest layer, closest to your spine. It consists of muscle fibers that encircle the torso. Contracting these muscles will stabilize the spine and pelvis. This layer attaches to your diaphragm and supports healthy breathing. This deepest layer is responsible for drawing the rest of the belly inward. This contraction feels like strong vines weaving around the body. Deepen the following abdominal contraction several times in a row.

- Inhale.

- Lengthen the sound of your exhalation as you contract your abdominals. Picture and feel your abdominals contracting like strong vines interweaving across each other.

### *Postural Muscles that Lie Beneath the Abdominal Wall: Iliopsoas and Multifidus*

These muscles work with the abdominals to anchor the lower back. This contraction feels like a vise pressing your navel toward your spine.

- Inhale.

- Exhale with a powerful breath sound to contract your abdominals. This feels like a vise spiraling your muscles toward your spine. Visualize a powerful vortex while corkscrewing the abdominals.

## The Five Steps of the Core Abdominal Foundation Formula

There are five steps to the Foundation Formula. Your goal is to blend each step into the next until you have completed all five steps. Don't relax the abdominals on the inhalation; the abdominals can then powerfully contract deeper and deeper on each exhale. Think of wrapping, carving, and tightening your abdominals to the exclusion of everything else.

## Step One of the Core Abdominal Foundation Formula

*Position:*

Sit on the floor on a mat. Your knees are bent; the soles of your feet are on the floor. Wrap your hands behind your thighs and draw your waist in and up.

Always isolate the hip and leg muscles before you begin. Keep them contracted for the entire Foundation Formula. They help you contract the deep abdominals. Tightly press your legs together. Continuously squeeze your buttocks muscles and

contract your pelvic floor area. The pelvic floor muscles surround the pubic bone, tailbone, and sit bones. (Find your pelvic floor muscles by coughing.) Draw these muscles together like a camera lens or shutter closing.

*Start:*

- Inhale.
- Exhale. Lengthen your exhalation as you contract your abdominals, moving backward into a deep C-curve. Your back takes on the shape of the letter C. Aim the back of your waist toward the floor. Look into your midsection.

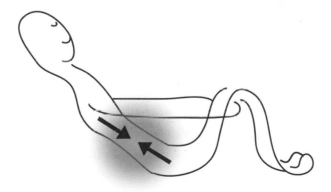

*Visual Imagery Guide—Step One, Core Abdominal Foundation Formula*

This step involves the outermost layer of your abdominals. These muscle fibers run vertically.

- Exhale while picturing the color red and vigorously contracting your abdominal muscles. This abdominal contraction feels like a clamshell clamping shut within the trunk. Your rib cage and pubic bone forcefully draw together into your waist.

- Inhale. Keep the abdominals contracted while returning to a sitting position. Continue with step two of the Core Abdominal Foundation Formula.

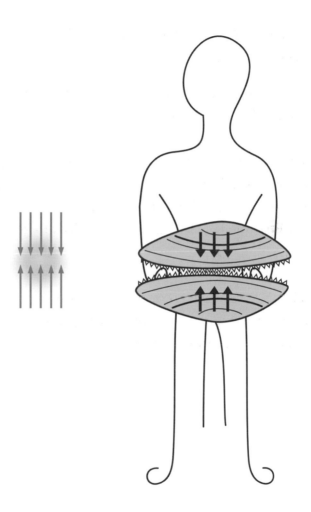

## Step Two of the Core Abdominal Foundation Formula

*Start:*

- Exhale forcefully as you contract your abdominals, moving backward again into your C-curve.

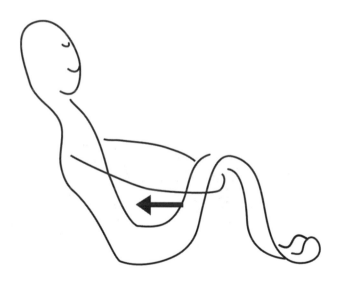

- Powerfully cinch your abdominals together.

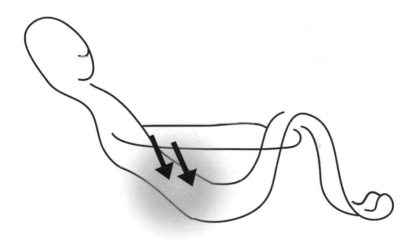

## Visual Imagery Guide—Step Two, Core Abdominal Foundation Formula

This step involves the external obliques. These muscle fibers run in diagonal slants. The abdominal contraction in step two feels like you are tightening and drawing the straps of a life jacket together.

- Picture the color orange as you visualize these straps attached in the front of your body to the bottom of your ribs. Exhale powerfully while feeling the life jacket forcefully pulled together, inward, and downward along the front of your body and toward your hips. Picture the life jacket as the abdominal muscles wrapping snuggly around your rib cage and then feel the contraction cinch your waist and hips.

- Inhale. Keep the abdominals contracted while returning to sitting and continue with step three of the Core Abdominal Foundation Formula.

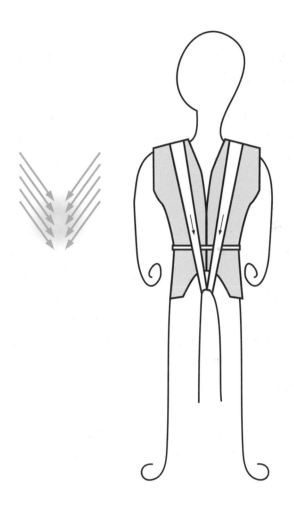

## Step Three of the Core Abdominal Foundation Formula

*Start:*

- Exhale powerfully as you contract your abdominals, moving backward again into your C-curve.

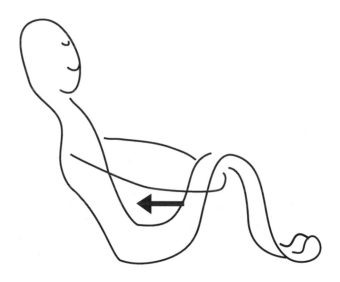

- Pull your abdominal muscles in and up.

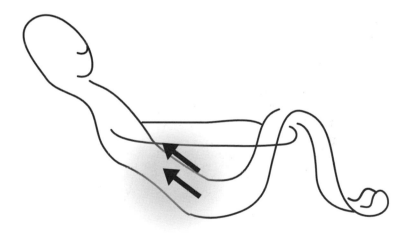

## Visual Imagery Guide—Step Three, Core Abdominal Foundation Formula

You are working on the third layer of the abdominals. The muscle fibers run in diagonal slants. They originate at the pelvic rim and insert into the last four ribs.

- Picture the color yellow while forcefully scooping your abdominal muscles in and up. Exhale while feeling the powerful elastic action of zippers drawing your abdominal wall back and up. The center of your body takes on a hollow, scooped-out bowl shape. Feel the powerful elastic sensation of the abdominals drawing away from your pubic bone, in toward your spine, and finally up and underneath your rib cage. This feels like you have hiked the waistband of your pants up to your armpits.

- Inhale. Return to a sitting position and keep your abdominals tight while you continue with step four of the Core Abdominal Foundation Formula.

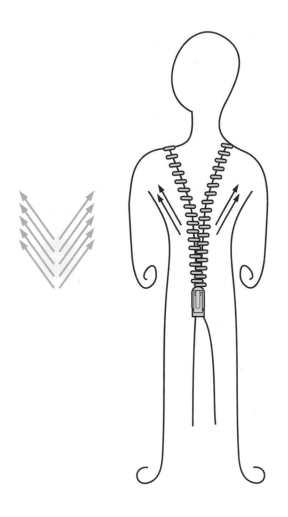

## Step Four of the Core Abdominal Foundation Formula

*Start:*

● Exhale strongly as you contract your abdominals, moving backward again into your C-curve.

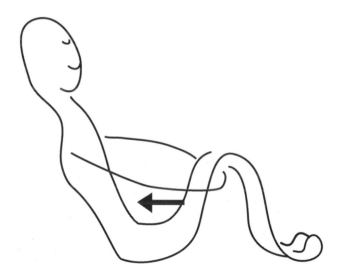

- Tightly wrap your abdominal muscles together.

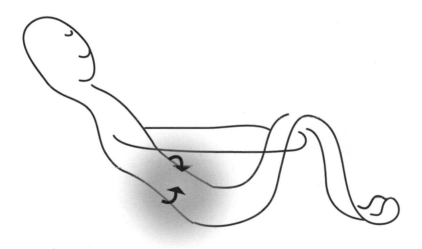

## Visual Imagery Guide—Step Four, Core Abdominal Foundation Formula

In this step, you are working on the fourth and deepest layer of your abdominals. The muscle fibers run horizontally.

- Picture the color green while powerfully wrapping your abdominal muscles together. This abdominal contraction feels like the powerful constricting motion of strong vines drawn together across your stomach. While exhaling, visualize your abdominal muscle fibers powerfully sliding and interweaving across each other. This feels like you are attempting to pull closed a tight coat.

- Inhale. Keep your abdominals tight while returning to sitting and continue with step five of the Core Abdominal Foundation Formula.

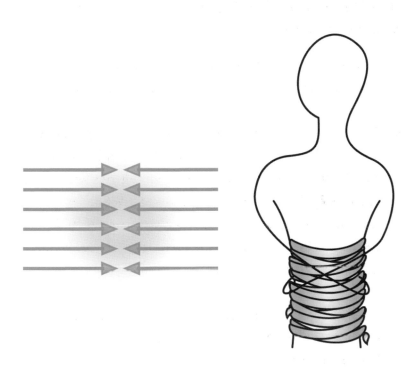

## Step Five of the Core Abdominal Foundation Formula

*Start:*

● Exhale as you contract your abdominals, moving backward into your C-curve.

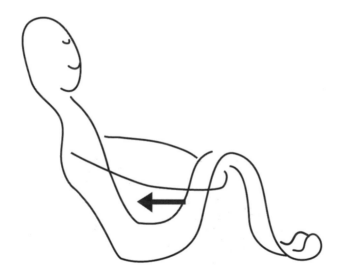

- Pull your abdominal muscles toward your spine.

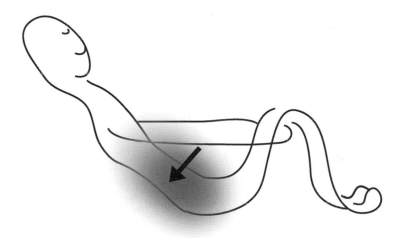

*Visual Imagery Guide – Step Five, Core Abdominal Foundation Formula*

This step is for the iliopsoas and multifidus muscles that lie beneath the abdominal wall. These muscles work with the abdominals to anchor the lower back.

- Picture the colors blue, indigo, and violet while forcefully sinking your abdominal muscles inward toward your spine.

- Exhale while sinking your abdominals toward your spine like a vise. Feel the vise as it flattens your abdominal muscles toward your back. The abdominals coil inward like a powerful vortex.

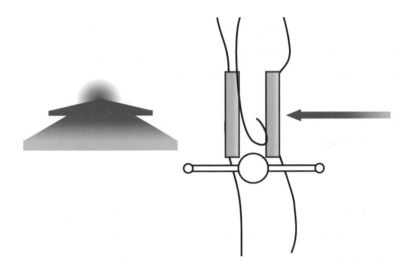

## Foundation Formula Success

Breathing, visual imagery, and colors help you to continuously contract the layers of your abdominals toward your spine. The abdominals feel like they have contracted through to your backbone. Drawing your upper legs together and squeezing your buttocks and pelvic floor muscles together help the abdominal contractions.

Memorize the five directions of the arrows, as pictured in the diagrams for the five steps. The arrows help you to picture the directional force of the abdominal muscular contractions.

Memorize the five images of the core abdominal Foundation Formula. While performing the five steps, keep repeating to yourself, "clam powerfully closing," "life jacket cinching," "zipper zipping," "vines tightening and weaving," and "vise clamping." Remember that each image characterizes the direction of the internal abdominal contraction. Picture the red clam, orange life jacket, yellow zipper, green vines, and blue/violet vise to strengthen the contractions. You may choose to repeat a step several times to feel the muscular contraction.

**Inhale. Exhale…**
Vertically clamp your
abdominals shut like a
red clamshell . . .

**Inhale. Exhale…**
Cinch your abdominals
diagonally, together and
downward like wearing an
orange life jacket . . .

**Inhale. Exhale…**
Tighten your abdominals in and
back like yellow zippers . . .

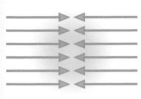

**Inhale. Exhale...**
Wrap your abdominal muscles
horizontally around your body
like constricting green vines . . .

**Inhale. Exhale...**
Sink and spiral your abdominals
towards your spine like a blue/
violet vise . . .

---

### Challenge

To target your deep postural muscles, reverse the five-step
Foundation Formula. This provides stability for your spine.

# Summary

The key to feeling centered lies within you, with breathing, massage, meditation, progressive relaxation, core strength, and stretching.

Conscious breath training prepares you to meet and address life's inevitable challenges. The benefits have vast and wide-reaching applications. Conscious breathing helps with child birthing, conquers developmental and emotional milestones, improves physical and mental healing, and ultimately can provide serenity at the end of life's journey. It is your right to take rich, full breaths with deep, primal breath sounds. Instead of holding your breath when you hoist yourself out of the car, lift something heavy, climb stairs, get a muscle cramp, work out at the gym, or take a medical test—breathe!

Breathing techniques and practice provide an essential tool to support you in times of need. People who have learned and practice breathing techniques can attest to their value. They have said, "Thank goodness I knew these breathing and core techniques before this difficult circumstance occurred in my life." "Why didn't I learn the importance of my core and efficient breathing as a child? I wish I had known about the benefits of conscious breathing techniques and core strength years ago. I could have also shared it with loved ones. They would have gotten through a tough experience quicker and with fewer residual problems."

Unfortunately, most of the population treats breathing as no more than an instinct or involuntary reflex. From our first breath to our last, what we do throughout our life's journey to impact our breathing leads to transformation. Experience your life from a rewarding, healthy, and efficient new perspective. Extend your breathing and body-care skills to all aspects of your life, including interpersonal relationships, physical activities, joys, successes, and challenges. You will experience life to the fullest with emotional equilibrium, mental acuity, and physical vitality.

# About the Author

**L**arkin Barnett is a Pilates-based physical-therapy and movement therapist with forty years of experience in teaching, choreographing, and performing for organizations such as Harvard University, Longy School of Music, and the University of Lappeenranta, Finland. She has been a professor of dance at Virginia Commonwealth University and a professor at Florida Atlantic University in the Exercise Science and Health Promotions department.

The series of adult and children's fitness books Larkin developed contain the three essential components for healthy—as well as special needs—children: conditioning, strength, and flexibility. Autism Speaks, the nation's largest autism science and advocacy organization, selected her books as resources for parents and professionals.

Larkin's several Pilates certifications include Polestar and specializations in golf Pilates. She received a BA in dance and drama from Sweet Briar College in Virginia and an MA in dance from Mills College in California. In 2007, the President's Council on Physical Fitness and Sports named her a President's Challenge Advocate.

Formerly a movement therapist and fitness professional at Canyon Ranch Spa, Larkin is now a national speaker on stress management, peak performance, and lung function.

### Related Quest Titles

*Breathe into Being*, by Dennis Lewis
*The Chakras and the Human Energy Fields*,
by Shafica Karagulla, with Dora van Gelder Kunz
*Feng Shui for the Body*, by Daniel Santos
*Neurospeak*, by Robert Masters
*The Way to Awaken*, by Robert Masters
*Yoga for Your Spiritual Muscles*, by Rachel Schaeffer

# Praise for Larkin Barnett's
## *Practical Centering*

"A powerful book that has the potential to transform lives."
**—Valerie Lipstein, Certified Coach and Consultant**

"These easy-to-follow exercises can make a difference in
our physical, mental, and emotional well-being."
**—Robert Volkmann, MD**

"Highly recommended for those who seek to make
great strides in their lives."
**—Brian W. Wright, Fitness Manager, Canyon Ranch**

"Self massage and using breathing muscles more efficiently
purifies the bloodstream and reduces toxic build-up. By practicing
the principles in this book, you will learn quick ways to reduce stress,
muscular tension and mental sluggishness, and factors related to
premature aging. You will also see improved sleep patterns
and complexion as you boost the immune system."
**—Jeannie Smith, LMP**

"As a young dancer struggling for stamina, Larkin had
a life-altering realization of the importance of proper breathing.
Now she is dedicated to improving our lives with her inspired
knowledge of strengthening body and spirit."
**—Steven Caras, Dancer and subject of the new
PBS television documentary,** *Steven Caras: See Them Dance*